A BOOT UP

THE CHILTERNS

Robert Wood

First published in Great Britain in 2011

British Library Cataloguing-in-Publication Data
A CIP record for this title is available from the British Library

ISBN 978 0 85710 046 7

PiXZ Books
Halsgrove House, Ryelands Business Park,
Bagley Road, Wellington, Somerset TA21 9PZ
Tel: 01823 653777
Fax: 01823 216796
email: sales@halsgrove.com

An imprint of Halstar Ltd, part of the Halsgrove group of companies
Information on all Halsgrove titles is available at: www.halsgrove.com

Printed and bound in China by Toppan Leefung Printing Ltd

idgewater Monument

Contents

How to use this book

The Area

The Chiltern Hills, designated as an Area of Outstanding Natural Beauty (AONB), remain a beautiful, unspoilt corner of England. The Chilterns regularly take the number 1 spot in polls of the best place to live in Britain. The rolling hills combine with beech woodland and chalk downs to provide a haven for wildlife. On the downs in summer are to be found abundant orchids and the rare Chilterns gentian. In the southern Chilterns the red kite is everywhere. And then there are the trees in autumn. Four nature reserves feature in the 10 walks.

As walking country goes the Chilterns are hard to beat. To the west there is a walk beside the Thames before it joins a section of the Shakespeare Way (Stratford left, the Globe right), while another walk drops in on a fine Elizabethan mansion before arriving in Henley's own Happy Valley with not a skiff in sight. More centrally, around the Wycombes, is Disraeli country: a visit is made to his house. The Hellfire Club was hereabouts too: just what did go on there? Further east a monument to a canal-builder to rival Nelson's Column suddenly rears up and there is a roller-coaster ramble to the north-west of Chesham, the first town in the Chilterns to be designated a *Walkers are Welcome* town. Add in at least three villages that film-makers have taken a shine to and, yes, the Chilterns are hard to beat.

The Routes

All routes are circular. They vary from $3\frac{1}{2}$ to $8\frac{1}{2}$ miles and are graded from one to three boots — from easy to more challenging. Routes are along public rights of way or occasionally unmarked but sanctioned tracks, or across open access land. Please remember that conditions under foot will vary greatly according to the season and the weather. Other than that all seasons have something going for them depending on taste; readers will have their own preferences. For me the Chilterns are especially appealing when the leaves start to fall.

This book is no different from others in assuming that the great majority of walkers will arrive by car.

The countryside is never free of danger but the greatest risk comes when crossing roads or walking alongside them or crossing a railway — rare, but one instance here.

The Maps

A map is needed to locate the starts and to check out the route. The sketch maps can only be a rough guide. Three Ordnance Survey maps are needed — Explorer 171, 172 and 181.

Good walking: I hope you enjoy the walks as much as I did. I hope to go back for more so look out for *A Boot Up More of the Chilterns*. For the time being let me thank those who came out walking with me — Jim Biggs, Sean and Anne Boyle, Elspeth Baillie and Rachel Wood.

Hambleden Valley

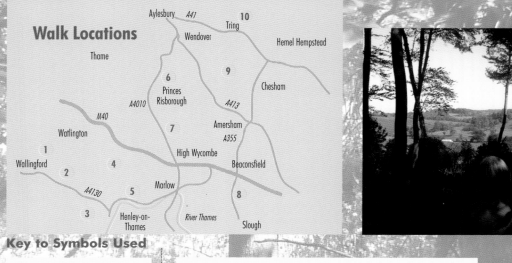

Walk Locations

Aylesbury *A41*
10
Tring
Wendover
Hemel Hempstead
Thame
6
9
Princes
Risborough
Chesham
A4010
M40
A413
Watlington
7
Amersham
1
A355
Wallingford
High Wycombe
2
4
Beaconsfield
A4130
5
Marlow
8
3
Henley-on-
Thames
River Thames
Slough

Key to Symbols Used

Level of difficulty:

Easy 🦋

Fair 🦋🦋

More challenging 🦋🦋🦋

Map symbols:

🚗 Park & start

Road

----- Footpath

■ Building / Town

+ Church

🪣 Pub

1 Britwell Salome and Swyncombe Downs

Wonderful views, opium poppy fields (what?), a former royal deer park, a fine open space; check them out in this rewarding six-mile ramble.

Leaving Britwell Salome the route heads south past Britwell House and its monuments before swinging east to pass Ewelme Park, once a royal deer park. Joining the Ridgeway the route turns north to pass the little church of St Botolph with its Crusader connections before climbing to skirt Swyncombe Downs where a detour is possible. The walk then returns through woodland to the start.

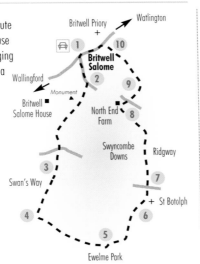

Level: 🌸 🌸
Length: 6½ miles
Terrain: Undulating with a pull up to Ewelme Park and a bigger pull up to the highest point of Swyncombe Downs, open country walking, some woodland walking, a little road walking
Park and Start: Britwell Salome, beside defunct telephone box (GR 672933). Approach from Wallingford or Watlington on the B4009
Map: OS Explorer 171
Websites: homepage.ntlworld.com/ clive.buckley/clive.buckley (re Ewelme Park) johnandsacha.com/swyncombe.html

7

① Cross over the busy B4009 to the side of The Goose and set off in the direction of Britwell Hill.

'Salome' is 'Sulham', like the Berkshire village; 'Britwell' is 'Brightwell'. The Goose attracted national attention when the latest of three Michelin-starred chefs quit in the face of calls for proper "pub grub" (and less in the way of foam sorbets).

Once past the end of the village the landscape opens out wonderfully, with superb views to the east. A bench thoughtfully supplied allows passers-by to take in some quintessential Chiltern scenery.

② Carry on along the road until you see a track going off to the right. Take it and very soon pass an attractive property called Monument Cottage. Beyond, and over to the right, is Britwell House and its grounds. As the house comes into view spot an object in front of it.

In 1764 Sir Edward Simeon built a monument to his parents in front of Britwell House. It was a column topped with an urn in the shape of a pineapple. This is the monument you can see. There is another to the north of the house over to the west of Monument Cottage.

Proceed along the track. Ahead of you

(according to season) is a riot of colour. Just what are these fields full of white and cream flowers, with the odd red bloom interspersed among them? It can't be, can it? Yes, it can. They are opium poppy fields. Stoned rabbits, you ask. How would anyone know?

Poppy growing on a commercial scale in this country dates from about nine years ago, prompted by a world-wide shortage of morphine – legally sourced, that is.

Over to the right is an iconic sight that became very familiar during the preparation of *A Boot Up the Berkshire Downs* – Didcot Power

Simeon's monument to his parents in front of Britwell House

Afghanistan in the Chilterns

Ewelme Park is a replica
of the Elizabethan house
which stood on this site until
destroyed by fire in 1913.
The park was once a
substantial Royal deer park.

Station. Turn left between two fields
of poppies to reach a road. There go
right for a short distance and then left
up a track.

(3) You are now on Swan's Way.
As to why *Swan's* Way, a fellow
walker and writer believes that the name
comes from the swan which forms the
centrepiece of the crest of Bucks County
Council. Nothing to do with Proust at all.

*Gorgeous white house
in Britwell Priory*

(4) At a crossing of tracks leave
Swan's Way and turn left
towards Ewelme Park. Carry on up the

track to reach a gate. At this point the
going gets steeper. As you ascend,
pause to look back to splendid views
across Oxfordshire. At the top of the field
Ewelme Park is just around the corner.

(5) At a crossing of tracks turn
left to join the Ridgeway.
Bear right past some stables to enter
a field to the right and then, shortly
afterwards, a field to the left. Follow
the field edge for a short while before
turning into a wood. Now the path
descends quite sharply. At the end of

the wood enter a field through a gate. Across the field is another gate. Once through it go right. The wall belongs to Swyncombe Manor, but you won't see it. As the wall turns into the drive there, over to the right, is the parish church of St Botolph, so tucked away you might easily miss it.

Swyncombe is derived from the Old English name of 'Swin', meaning wild boar, and 'cumb', meaning the valley in the flank of the hill. The eleventh century church is dedicated to the seventh century patron saint of gateways and/or travelling St Botolph. Inside are votive crosses thought to have been painted by medieval knights leaving for the Crusades.

Ewelme Park

6 Go up the road past the old rectory to reach a crossroads. Ahead of you is the track that is going to take you around the side of Swyncombe Downs. To the left are those same fine views across Oxfordshire.

7 Go down and then up to enter a wooded section. Carry on through the woods before the track starts to descend. On the left there is an obvious track; in fact an earthwork thought to have been an ancient boundary. If you wanted to detour onto the Downs you could follow the earthwork. As you round the bottom of the Downs there in the middle distance is Britwell House, monument and all. Continue along the track until you reach North End Farm.

8 Go right along the farm drive to reach a road. Cross the road and carry on until a signpost comes up.

9 Over in the distance vehicles can be seen moving. They are on the M40. The track you want lies in woodland apart from briefly emerging at an intersection of fields.

10 Once the road is visible at Cooper's Farm you can — by turning left along farm tracks that run parallel to the road — avoid some of the road walking (it isn't far but the road is busy). Then turn right off the tracks when you spot a gorgeous white house opposite and walk up the road to the car.

View east towards the end of the walk

2 Nettlebed and Russell's Water

A handsome reminder of the industrial and pre-industrial past, a flagship nature reserve, a stunning park, echoes of the film Enduring Love and another location with filmic resonance, all combined with some of the best scenery the Chilterns can offer.

Level: ❤

Length: 6 miles

Terrain: Undulating; descents into valleys, ascents up the other sides; a little road walking

Park and Start: Nettlebed, by the green (GR 701867)

Approach from Wallingford or Henley

Map: OS Explorer 171

Websites: www.nettlebed.org.uk/Brick. History

www.bixandassendon.org.uk/placesof interest2

www.stonor.com/home

www.youtube.com/watch?v=KwSCFfHHV3M

The walk starts in Nettlebed, not far from Henley. As the route wends through Warburg Nature Reserve it enters a dry valley bottom before rising to join the Oxfordshire Way. Some exquisite scenery follows with the inevitable red kites as company.

The route then turns west to arrive at the village of Russell's Water, home of a large duck pond where a rather famous film was shot. A descent followed by a level section followed by an ascent concludes the ramble.

Russell's Water · Duck Pond · **7** · **Pishill** · **6** · **5** · Stonor Park · **8** Warburg Nature Reserve · **4** · ■ Lodge Farm · **Stonor** · **3** · **9** · **2** · **Nettlebed** · Old Kiln · **1** · ■ Soundess House · A4130 Wallingford · ✚ · 🚌 · Henley

2

Old Kiln in Nettlebed

Nettlebed and Russell's Water

14

(1) Before or after the walk have a look at the Old Kiln, which is just around the corner from where you are parked.

Set off in a north-easterly direction along Chapel Lane. At a sign go left in the direction of 'Magpies' but do not branch off to that house; rather stay on the lane. At a crossroads stop to view the mansion over to the right, Soundess House.

(2) Continue by the side of a wood before entering Warburg Nature Reserve. Very soon a display board clues you in to what this treasure has to offer. Continue

> *Nettlebed was the major centre for brick, tile and pottery manufacture in Oxfordshire from medieval times, and possibly even earlier, up until the twentieth century. Situated on the crest of the Chilterns escarpment on a rich bed of Reading Clay and with a plentiful supply of firewood and spring water, Nettlebed was a natural site for brick and pottery making.*

> *Soundess House existed in 1535 and probably for some time before. It is recorded that in 1665 Nell Gwynne was sent by the King to stay at Soundess House to escape the Great Plague.*

Soundess House

down through the reserve until arriving at a path running across you, evidently occupying a dry valley. Turn right but then almost immediately left to go uphill through a smart new gate marked 'Wildlife Walk'. The track soon levels out to reveal, to left and right, an enchanting flat stretch of green sward.

(3) Go along the stretch to the right about as far as you can go before turning left to go uphill. When the track levels out the temptation is to turn left and continue on the Wildlife Walk but to do so would be to go in the wrong direction. Continue uphill and bear right to exit from the nature reserve.

(4) You are on the Oxfordshire

In Warburg Reserve

Warburg Nature Reserve comprises a mix of chalk grassland and ancient woodland, which makes it an ideal site for birds and butterflies. Over 2,000 species of plant, animal and fungus have been recorded here.

Way. Ahead is Lodge Farm. Skirt round it on the right and enter a field to the left. Stay on the field edge until a path across the field beckons. Cross the field into a wood. Carry on down the wood until a road is reached. Cross over and very soon when a track comes in from the left go half left and proceed through the wood before emerging into an open space. Over to the right is the magnificent Stonor Park. And there is the definitive Chilterns signature – the ubiquitous red kites.

(5) Go up the field to a meeting of tracks. If a detour to the pub in Pishill is on your mind - the pub is the Crown, which at least two respected judges recommend – all you need to do is to walk down the lane that runs

The same family has occupied Stonor Park for over 850 years (no wonder with that scenery). The opening scene of the film of Ian McEwan's Enduring Love, where the balloon accident occurs, is set in the Chilterns and could easily have been shot here (in fact it was shot in the Wormsley Estate further east).

up from the road to Pishill House (it is still the Oxfordshire Way). You will find the pub on your left.

6 Otherwise turn left at the junction and proceed for a mile or so, gradually ascending, until some farm buildings come up on the left. Once clear of the buildings cross over to join the lane running west. Continue past Upper Nuttall's Farm staying on the lane until the village of Russell's Water comes into view. The first thing you will see is Russell's Water's claim to fame: a rather large duck pond. Anyone who saw the 1968 film *Chitty Chitty Bang Bang* will remember a pond that Truly Scrumptious drove into more than once. Well, this is it. The bench is a useful prop. The fish and ducks will

Above Pishill

Duck pond

devour any bits of sandwich you have left over.

7 Turn left at the road junction and in a hundred yards or so, just before the green, take a way-marked track off to the right. Follow the track down to the bottom and turn left. Ignore the first five-way junction to arrive

at another (709884) with Westwood Manor Farm visible to the right.

8 Continue in the same direction across a field to reach a wood. Veer slightly right to pick up the edge of the wood and head uphill on the grass before joining a gravel track that will take you past Soundess

Farm and return you to where you were earlier opposite Soundess House.

9 Turn right and return to Nettlebed the way you came. If you didn't look at the puddlestone in the shelter area before you left you might want to do so now and the display board close by it.

3 **Greys Court and Friar Park**

A fine Tudor house and gardens, a golf course set in beautiful parkland, George Harrison's last residence and a glorious stroll along Henley's own Happy Valley.

Leaving the village of Rotherfield Greys the walk passes through woodland to Greys Court, a splendid mansion with strong Elizabethan connections. The spirit of place is palpable. A trail through an ancient wood leads to a beautiful golf course. Now in the outskirts of Henley the next feature is quirky – a 120 room mansion once the home of the Beatle George Harrison. Henley has a Happy Valley? It surely does. Who would

Level:
Length: 6 miles
Terrain: Field and parkland paths, drives and tracks, limited road walking with only one busy stretch and that is short
Park and Start: Rotherfield Greys, outside the church (GR 726824)
Map: OS Explorer 171

have guessed that within two miles of Henley, for so many of us synonymous with the regatta and the Thames, there would be scenery like this?

1 Just before the Maltsters Arms turn left and follow a footpath alongside the churchyard, making for the stile ahead. Head across the field to another stile and pass through the gap in the hedge. Veer half-right across the next field and hop over a stile to join a path.

2 Turn right and pass between trees and high hedges. The path becomes a track and passes alongside a golf course before crossing a drive to a gate. Continue ahead to reach a road.

3 Turn right and follow the road until you come to a cricket pitch. Head for a footpath at the other side of the pitch just to the right of the pavilion. Go down the rutted track, cross a stile and descend through a wooded section to the next stile before making for another stile at the bottom of the field. On the other side of the lane is a short rise that leads to another stile. Greys Court is straight ahead. The ambience is pure Chilterns; green and rolling with red kites swooping and wheeling.

Rotherfield means "cattle lands". The nearest market was Henley, already in the fourteenth century an important market for supplying London, especially with grain and wood, and much of the local produce was probably sold there.

The mainly Tudor-style Greys Court was once owned by Sir Francis Knollys, treasurer to Elizabeth I and jailer of Mary, Queen of Scots. The interior is still furnished as a family home. Within the gardens is a medieval fortified tower of 1347 that affords extensive views of the gardens and the surrounding countryside.

4 Keeping the house to your left head towards a line of pines. Veer right and proceed through 'Johnnies Gate' before skirting a pond to your right. A corrugated barn is over to the left. Head for it and cross the stile. At a minor road turn right and look for a path to the left that is going to take you through a wood,

Greys Court

Jim by Johnnnie's Gate at Greys Court

JOHNNIE'S GATE

trees. Enter it by stepping over a double-logged affair. As always when crossing golf courses take a little time to assess the lie of the land and in particular where the route posts sit. Here you need to bear ever so slightly right and head up towards some trees. Savour the setting as you go; it is quite superb. The exit from the course can be spotted quite clearly

Lambridge Wood. Walking through it is rather soothing and restful.

(5) At a junction of paths turn right and continue through the woods until ahead of you Badgemore Park golf course beckons.

(6) Badgemore Park is a beautiful parkland course enhanced by a collection of mature specimen

Badgemore Park golf course

over to the left. Emerge onto a road and go past a des res colony until some razor-wire on a fence to the right alerts you to a property that resonates – Friar Park.

(7) It is not possible to circum-navigate the Friar Park estate. Where the path is blocked, drop down to an estate road and turn right. At Badgemore Primary School turn right and go uphill for a short way to re-establish contact with Friar Park. It is not possible to see into the grounds but at least you can admire the main gates that are adjacent to the Henley-Rotherfield road.

(8) Cross the road to Paradise Road. At a three-way junction carry on straight ahead. The lane is

Friar Park is the 120 room Victorian neo-Gothic mansion bought by the Beatle George Harrison in January 1970. The mansion was largely open to the public until the murder of John Lennon in New York in December 1980 caused the gates to be locked, and the aforesaid fences and video cameras to be installed. Those did not stop an intruder breaking into the residence on December 30, 1999, attacking Harrison and his wife and leaving Harrison with a punctured lung, seven stab wounds, and head injuries. Diagnosed with cancer he died in November 2001 aged 58.

going to curve up to the right towards Henley College but you are going to go down by the left of a house to reach a fork in the track (754823). The choice is easy: follow the 'Rotherfield Greys 1¾ miles' signpost.

Happy Valley

(9) The path rises slightly until it crosses Pack and Prime Lane (wonderful name). This closing section is quite sublime, especially with the sun low in the sky. With some justification the locals call it 'Happy Valley'. The house up ahead is Lower Hernes. After a couple of stiles the track leaves Happy Valley and begins to rise up slightly. At a junction where every-

Rotherfield Greys cricket pitch

thing to the left is 'Private' hop over the stile to the right and continue along the field edge until a stile comes up on the left. Once over it head up the incline to the left to reach level ground where Rotherfield Greys, and in particular the Maltsters Arms, is visible. If you have been anticipating refreshment, and the time is right, it is only five minutes away.

Author on last leg (not legs)

4 **Turville and Ibstone**

A classic English village that film-makers adore; a house in the next village that is home to opera every September; views to make you gasp: it's the Chilterns in a nutshell; if you only have two hours to spare this is the one.

Turville is perhaps best known as the location for the TV series *The Vicar of Dibley*, and also

for its iconic windmill where the family in *Chitty Chitty Bang Bang* lived. The route proceeds directly to Fingest where, on leaving the village, it passes a house that hosts an opera company every September. It then continues over open ground before climbing to the village of Ibstone. After a quick peek at what can be seen of Ibstone House, a villa that has had interesting

owners, the route descends through a wood and, once into the open, offers sublime views over Turville and the surrounding countryside.

Level: 🥾
Length: 3½ miles
Terrain: Flattish, one climb, one descent; a little road walking
Park and Start: Turville, by the church (GR 767912) Approach from Watlington or from Henley
Map: OS Explorer 171
Websites: www.helenanddouglas.org.uk/events/49/fingest-great-barn-opera

4 Turville and Ibstone

25

1 On the north side of the green locate the Chiltern Way signs. As you go between two houses your attention will immediately be grabbed by a windmill on the skyline.

The route does not climb up to the windmill but instead turns right to go through one gate and then another before heading up a stretch of broad sward to reach a stile. There follows a wooded section interrupted by a little road until a church comes into view.

Fingest churc

The windmill is Cobstone Mill, an eighteenth-century smock mill but not operational since the First World War. It featured in a 1976 episode of The New Avengers television series in which Purdey and Gambit drive through the village in a yellow MGB, chasing a helicopter that lands by the windmill. And in Chitty Chitty Bang Bang the family lived in the windmill.

This is Fingest church. Proceed down the path to reach a road and you are in the pretty village of Fingest.

2 Walk up the little road past the church. After 400 yards or so Manor Farm appears on the right.

The village name of Fingest comes from the Anglo-Saxon Thinghurst, meaning 'wooded hill where assemblies are made'. It is easy to see how with frequent pronunciation 'Tinghurst' became 'Tingest' and you don't have to be a cockney to know how quickly 'Ting' can become 'Fing'.

In the wood

veers to the right continue in that direction. Follow the field edge, at one point skirting a wood, before arriving at a path that goes off to the

Peering into the Manor Farm complex a huge mounted clock catches the eye but also a large barn, which figures given that Great Barn opera puts on opera productions at this venue. Perhaps the big blue clock was a prop used in a film.

Just up the road, and shortly after a path comes in from the right, the road bends. Leave the road and take a track off to the left. This spot is called 'Gravesend' on the map, but it is far from clear why. Certainly there is nothing to see.

 Go up the track and where it

There is a connection between Gravesend and Fingest for what it is worth. In 1163 the manor of Fingest was given to the Bishop of Lincoln and was used as the country residence for the Lincoln diocese. It is recorded that Richard of Gravesend, Bishop of Lincoln, stayed at Fingest several times in the late 1200s.

right (to Harecramp Cottages). Shortly afterwards there is a path to the left which climbs straight up to the ridge. Do not take this path but continue into some woods (the path will be very muddy after heavy rain) until a bridleway is signed diagonally off to the left.

4 Follow the bridleway as it winds upwards, using the white arrows on trees as a guide. On reaching a farm track turn left and proceed up the track, which soon becomes a metalled lane (the farm to the left is Twigside Farm; next to a property development). For a wonderful view turn around and look back over to the north-west. At a fork in the lane go left by the side of what turns out to be the village school to arrive at a road. You are in Ibstone, formerly Ipstone.

Ibstone House

5 Turn left past the school and at a junction take the road to the left where, over to the left, stands Ibstone House.

6 Look for a path off to the right of the road. Follow the path through the wood always in a downwards left-veering direction, using the way signs where posted. Watch out for deer. They were seen on the day of the walk. Having emerged

View to north-west from Ibstone

Ibstone House is a grade II listed eighteenth century villa with apparently sumptuous appointments, all set in the 428 acre estate gardens. A recent owner was ex-boxer Sol Kerzner, a peripatetic South African hotel and gambling tycoon. During the Second World War the place was owned by the author Rebecca West whose output was prodigious but is perhaps best known for her 10 year affair with H G Wells.

from the wood, and at a junction of paths, take the path to the right

House in Turville

which – progress through the field being barred – almost immediately turns left to follow a fence. The outlook is sensational but do watch out for the barbed wire.

(7) When the path runs out cross a stile and head across a field to another stile. After negotiating a sliver of woodland pass through a gate and almost immediately through another to the right. To regain Turville descend to a house; go through a gate and down some steps, and finally through a garden gate to reach a road. Turn left to pass the church of St Mary the Virgin which of course features in *The Vicar of Dibley*. The tiny cottage by the entrance to the church doubles as the vicar's home.

Old Vicarage, Turville

Turville church

5 Hambleden and the River Thames

An amble beside the River Thames followed by classic Chilterns woodland walking: what could be better?

Starting south of the village of Hambleden the route soon reaches the Thames. If a lazy saunter by the river is your fancy feel free. There is much to look at, from a handsome mansion across the river to the swans to the variety of boats and boaters and the general messing about on the river. After Medmenham Abbey, with its Hellfire Club connections, the route turns inland to reach the outskirts of Marlow where it joins a newish national walk, Shakespeare's Way. With the spirit of the Bard in tow the walk arrives at a site used in the Great War for training troops that exercises the imagination. After more woodland stretches the route emerges into the open, with superb views to the south and west. Hambleden is down below. What a stunning location it is. Certainly film-makers think so.

Level: 🥾🥾
Length: 8 miles
Terrain: Woodland, river meadows, some road walking mostly along lanes
Park and Start: A car park between Mill End and Hambleden (GR 785856)
Map: The walk starts on OS Explorer 171 and continues on OS Explorer 172
Websites: www.sas.com/offices/europe/uk/corporate/wittington.pdf
www.shakespearesway.org
www.chilternsaonb.org/place_details.asp?siteID=717

Turn right and proceed to the road junction at Mill End. Take the Marlow road but quite quickly turn right into Ferry Lane. At the bottom of the lane turn left. The Thames is now visible. Continue along the lane past the imposing Hambleden Place.

 After going through a gate immediately turn right and walk along the field edge towards the river. Proceed for 200 yards or so passing a charming house to the right (built 1897) before arriving at the river.

 Turn left along the river bank and continue for a mile and a half to a gate, enjoying as you go the activity on the river — and off it. Two fine houses can be seen on the other side of the river. Once through the gate look for the site of a defunct ferry crossing (there is a monument to your left).

 Turn left up a lane (you have no option). On your right is Medmenham Abbey, a location that resonates.

Go up the lane for a short while before veering off right at a footpath sign. Cross two stiles and enter a water meadow. At the far corner of the meadow is a cottage (Abbey Lodge). Note the mind-boggling glass and steel extension. Emerge onto the cottage drive and go up to the road.

 The road is busy but you are only on it for a couple of

Moored for the day

Medmenham Abbey was leased by Sir Francis Dashwood of West Wycombe and was the scene of the activities of the Hellfire Club from 1755 to 1763 before it migrated to West Wycombe (see walk 7). In truth nothing is known for sure about the identity of the 'nuns' who apparently frolicked in the grounds of the Abbey but it is said there was a motto above the entrance to the Abbey which declared "Do as you please".

minutes before diving down to the right. The house on the left, West Lodge, is thought to have been built to a design by Pugin. Have a chuckle at the gold-spangled gates (if closed). Carry on down this minor road past the Danesfield RAF Water Sports Centre (!) until the weirs of Hurley Lock come into view. That object lying in the grass: what could that be? It is an old capstan.

Immediately after passing Kingfisher Lodge go left up a steep incline that

Before locks with two lock gates were introduced, weirs with just one gate were used. The gate was left shut to increase the depth of water above it but had to be opened to let boats through, and those heading upstream had to be hauled up against the current using the capstan.

The capstan at Hurley Lock

you will not have been expecting. To your left is the huge Danesfield Estate but on the other side of the wall are the extensive grounds of Wittington House and Estate, now the home of the SAS Institute. At the top of the incline lies another surprise - a tunnel.

Once through the tunnel and by the end of a flint wall turn right and follow the path up to a gate. With Harleyford Golf Club to your left continue onwards, skirting the club house to arrive at East Lodge at the entrance to the club. Now walk up to

Follow the Bard
the Henley-Marlow road.

6 Cross the busy road and go right for 100 yards or so until you come to the first road off to the left. Go up the road and take the foot-

Shakespeare's Way is a recent creation. It runs from Stratford-on-Avon to the Globe Theatre in London. From Marlow it goes down to the Thames and thence to London and the Wooden O.

path off to the right. You are now on something called Shakespeare's Way and have been since the main road.

Veering away from the woods over to your right continue until you meet a track coming in from the right.

7 Go left across some open ground before entering woodland. Carry on through these woods until you reach a road. You are now on the Chiltern Way and you will stay

Wittington House was built in 1898 for the tea tycoon Hudson Ewbanke Kearley, later Viscount Devonport. He had the tunnel built so that he and his family could stroll in the grounds without being spied on by walkers and the like. There are inevitably tales of a ghost called – wouldn't you just know? – the 'grey lady'.

on it (coinciding with Shakespeare's Way) until Hambleden. Across the road you will have noticed a display board. It tells a surprising story - of how the wood to the left was put to use during World War One.

8 Carry on in the same direction through first more woodland and then open ground. Cross a road into Homefield Wood and continue until the track suddenly bears right, before long almost doubling back on itself (805871). Follow the path south for a short distance until it

reaches a road. Turn right and at a stile on the left cross into a field. Ahead is a farm – Rotten Row Farm.

9 Skirt the farm – admiring the duck pond and the duck house – before taking a track off to the right. Glorious views of Hambleden Valley

Duck house

Remarkably, Pullinghill Wood contains an intricate trench system that was used in training troops before they left for France. The troops were billeted in nearby Bovingdon Green camp on the other side of Marlow Common.

start to open up and soon you are at the edge of Hambleden village. Ahead is a cricket pitch set against a backdrop of old properties and, above them, serried clumps of trees filling the hillside. It is a magnificent sight. Turn right past the handsome Manor House and then left past the Stag and Huntsman. With the church to your right you are in the centre of the village.

Hambleden was the home of the original W.H.Smith. The village has often been used as a film location – check out Nanny McPhee and the Big Bang, Chitty Chitty Bang Bang (see also walks 2 and 4), 101 Dalmatians, Band of Brothers and Sleepy Hollow.

(10) Leaving the village stores to your right cross a bridge over the Hamble Brook and take the path to your left. Walk across the meadow parallel to the main road until you reach another old bridge. Here go up to a lane, turn right and, at the road, right again. Your car is over to the right.

Hambleden village stores

Howzat!

6 Whiteleaf Hill and Chequers

An ancient place with scintillating views; two nature reserves; the PM's country residence; magnificent tree-filled panoramas; well worth the time and effort.

Starting at Whiteleaf Hill high above Princes Risborough the walk proceeds through a nature reserve with experimental leanings to arrive at a vantage point offering the first views of Chequers (once referred to as 'Blair's Lair'). Passing through Chequers Estate (but only just) the route veers south-east through a wood containing a fine mix of trees, young and old, before turning west to return to the start.

Level: 🥾 🥾
Length: 5½ miles
Terrain: Undulating; in and out of woods; minimal road walking
Park and Start: Whiteleaf Hill car park; from Monks Risborough take the A4010 to Aylesbury, shortly turning right onto Peters Lane; near the top of the hill on the left is the car park (GR 823036)
Map: OS Explorer 181
Websites: www.ukattraction.com/east-of-england/brush-hill-nature-reserve
www.kophillclimb.org.uk

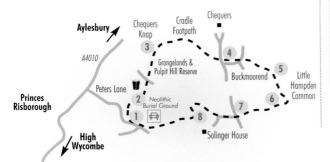

① Take the path beyond the display board that leads to an obvious path going right. Take that path. To the left (hard to spot, deliberately so) are the First World War trenches mentioned on the display board (used for the same purposes as in walk 5). Once through the gate you are on Whiteleaf Hill. To your left is a Neolithic burial mound and below the rim of the hill (you cannot see it) is Whiteleaf Cross. And there are always those sensational views.

Neolithic burial mound

coming in from the right. Cross over and very shortly pick up a path off to the right. At the top of an incline there are two gates. Take the gate over to the left and enter Grangelands and Pulpit Hill Nature Reserve. Follow

Grangelands and Pulpit Hill Nature Reserve

② To the right pick up the white acorn denoting the Ridgeway. You will be following the acorn for a while. Go through a gate and descend through a wood to emerge at a road and a pub, the Plough at Cadsden. Once past the pub be aware of a road

the path up through the reserve towards two gates. The management of this reserve has taken on the task of revitalising the cultivation of juniper, something that might already have begun when you visit.

③ On passing through the second gate continue upwards towards a gate at the top of the slope. Here turn right. Up to your left is a feature called Chequers Knap. Continue upwards to reach open space and follow the Ridgeway path alongside the fence, climbing to a kissing gate beside a metal gate at the brow of the hill. This delightful stretch is known as Cradle Footpath. Pass through a further gate at the other side of the field, turning slightly right, and continue with woodland on the

Chequers

Chequers is essentially a Tudor manor house built (or possibly rebuilt) in 1565. It was presented to the nation in 1917 by Lord Lee of Fareham. At the time a waggish peer suggested that if a Prime Minister was doing his job properly he wouldn't have time for weekends in the country. Of course the house has witnessed many world leaders attending conferences or on state visits.

right and a field on the left. You are looking for Chequers, the official country residence of the Prime Minister, and it soon comes up on the left. At the end of the wood, turn sharp left and follow the fence down-hill to go through two gates and cross the Chequers drive (note the camera surveillance).

4 Go ahead through a gate opposite and follow the fence to a road at Buckmoorend. Watch out especially for traffic from the right. Take the track opposite that goes up through a belt of trees. At a junction of paths say goodbye to the white acorns and turn right to join the South Bucks Way. Follow the track gradually uphill, all the while veering to the left. Pass through some young trees

followed by mature beechwood and, to your left, a mixed plantation including young conifers. At a way-mark take the narrow path that forks left to emerge at the junction of several paths.

5 At this point (864045), there is a choice of paths but the one to take is the Icknield Way Trail by the side of the field to your right. Follow the field edge until a sign directs you to leave the field but not for long because the first path to the right very soon brings you back to the edge of the same field.

6 Now you are heading west towards a wood. Halfway down the field a sign invites you to enter the next field. Continue down alongside the wood looking out for a sign that will send you into the wood. Go down through the wood bearing left at a junction until you emerge into open space with a house below you and a road up above. Skirt the house using the permissive footpath and go up the farm road to the road.

7 Opposite is a private road to Solinger House but it is also a public footpath. Where the road curves off to the left take a signed path into a field. Hugging the hedge carry on for a few hundred yards admiring the stands of trees over to the right until you reach an intersection of fields more or less in line with some buildings over to the right. Here go left up the hill. The house you can see to the left, just before you enter the wood (836034), is Solinger House.

8 Proceed through the wood ignoring tracks off to left and right. Finally, at the end of the wood, turn left and go up to a gate that leads to a farm road. Go right up the road and at a gate go left to reach Peters Lane. From there it is a short distance along the road to the car park. If circumstances permit you might want to visit Brush Hill Local Reserve opposite the car park; maybe also drive down Kop Hill — the road you passed at the top of the hill — scene of annual road climb races.

7 Bradenham and West Wycombe

Two fine mansions on a six-mile walk? It could be three if you like. What about a cave complex of scandalous repute and an awesome mausoleum set high on a hill? Add in a Chilterns backdrop and you have a walk to savour.

Starting in Bradenham, a beautiful National Trust village of which the centre-piece is Bradenham Manor once home to Isaac D'Israeli the father of Benjamin (see walk 9), the route proceeds through woodland before dropping into Hughenden Valley and Hughenden Manor, bought by Benjamin Disraeli in 1848 the year his father died. Then it is on to West Wycombe with its tempting menu of optional extras - West Wycombe Park, the Hellfire Caves, St Lawrence's church and the Mausoleum. From near the summit of West Wycombe Hill with its stellar views it remains to cross the railway before returning through woodland to Bradenham.

Level: ♥ ♥
Level: Two boots
Length: 6 miles (but more if extras in West Wycombe are taken on)
Terrain: A mixture of woodland and open spaces; some road walking; one shortish steep climb and another lesser climb
Park and Start: Bradenham, which is just off the A4010; in the small car park on the opposite side of the road from the church (GR 827973)
Map: OS Explorer 172
Websites: www.hellfirecaves.co.uk
www.westwycombeestate.co.uk
www.nationaltrust.org.uk/main/w-hughen-denmanor. (Be sure to use these sites to check opening times)

adenham
Bradenham Manor
Hughenden Manor
Downley
West Wycombe

Bradenham Manor

1 After surveying the church and Bradenham Manor, and checking out the display board, follow the track round the southern garden wall of the Manor to enter Bradenham Wood.

Bradenham Wood has been designated a site of special scientific interest (SSSI). Much of the woodland above the village is beech, planted in the 1800s by the local furniture industry.

2 Without deviating (just keep to the blue bridleway signs) look out for the next display board which is just over to the left. The subject is Naphill Common which is where you are standing. Carry on until you reach a T-junction of tracks.

3 Turn right and again follow the blue signs. At a farm road (Cookshall Farm) turn left and then bear right to come across another of those display boards that the National Trust does so well.

4 Take the minor road. Halfway uphill two footpath signs are apparent. Follow the obvious track downhill into Hughenden Valley. Just before a gate leading to a field a track runs across you. Turn left and after a short climb turn right at the top. Now you are overlooking that field. Carry on past a track coming in from the right (you will return down it) to make the gentle ascent to an

Hughenden Manor

estate road. Hughenden Manor is then to your left.

(5) Return the way you came and at the fork go downhill. At the bottom go right: you are now opposite the higher track where you were earlier. Enter some woods and before long reach a five-way junction. There go slightly left and then slightly right and uphill until an old house comes up - inscription 'Well House, 1813'. You are now in the village of Downley. At the end of the drive

Hughenden Manor was the home of Benjamin Disraeli, Queen Victoria's favourite Prime Minister, from 1848 to 1881. He was Dizzy to his wife Mary Anne if not to the Queen and inside the house are his personal effects. Outside is the formal garden that was re-created based on Mary Anne's original designs.

follow the road left up to an intersection. Around to the left, opposite the defunct Post Office, is a handy bench.

(6) Follow the signed path on the other side of the road and quite soon a school comes up on the right. Leaving it behind bear slightly right all the while aiming for the far corner of the housing development. Once through the gap cross a green to reach another gap. When a turn to the left appears take it. At the bottom turn right and continue along the road until the end. At a little road called 'Sunnycroft' go left down a path to enter an open space. There can be few better views of High Wycombe; above all the green dome of St Mary and St George, often mistaken for a mosque.

Hughenden Manor gardens

Built in 1765 the vast hexagonal monument is the final resting place for members of the Dashwood family. Behind it is the 18th century church of St Lawrence, with its golden ball on top (actually made of copper). The ball is visible for miles and apparently is big enough to hold up to eight people, and is said to have been used for secret meetings.

Old pump in Church Lane

(7) Ignore the track going downhill and instead enter a wood. After some twists and turns arrive at a gate where you might just want to catch your breath. For up on the hill is a marvellous spectacle - the Dashwood Mausoleum.

(8) Descend to a gate and join a little road. Go left under the railway bridge to reach the A4010. Cross the road and bear left and then right in the direction of West Wycombe. Carry on along the pavement past a church (advertising Anglican and Serbian Orthodox services but not at the same time). You are looking for a right turn into Church Lane. Should you wish to visit the Hellfire Caves the entrance is further along on the right through a garden

West Wycombe House and what became known as the Hellfire Caves were built by Sir Francis Dashwood in 1750-2 as a charitable act using unemployed local labour. Later Dashwood and other dilettantes and literati formed a club which a London paper dubbed the Hellfire Club. The club attracted much notoriety during its day – there were rumours of orgies and black magic and all sorts of goings on (see the reference to Medmenham Abbey in walk 5) – but once the club had disbanded the Hellfire Caves quickly fell into disrepair. It is said that hearts of Hellfire Club members were interred in the Mausoleum.

centre. The entrance to West Wycombe Park and House is on the other side of the road.

(9) The entrance to Church Lane may look like a courtyard but beyond is a lane. Just inside on the left is a workshop that still makes furniture using local beech wood. Climb up the lane and where a road comes in continue on to find a path off to the right.

(10) Before entering the field notice some steps over to the left. These will take you to the Mausoleum and St Lawrence's church should you wish to visit. Once into the field walk parallel to the road until you see a path stretching ahead of you at half right that crosses the field

White house on Bradenham Green

to the A4010 before going up to the railway.

(11) The railway must be crossed by foot so the order of the day is stop, look and listen. Before entering the wood look back over to West Wycombe Hill where the golden ball should be visible above the trees.

Climb up through the woodland and at a junction sporting yellow footpath signs veer left and continue along the track without dropping down until the garden wall of Bradenham Manor comes into view. Depending on the time, refreshment can be had at the Red Lion including home-made pies.

8 Hedgerley and Bulstrode Park

A picturesque village, an RSPB reserve, a wonderful open space, an Iron Age camp close by, an over-the-top Gothic mansion and a proper country pub; here is a short walk to lift the spirits.

Level: ♥

Length: 4 miles

Terrain: Woods and open space

Park and Start: Outside the White Horse Hedgerley which is off the A355 about four miles north of Slough (GR 968872)

Map: OS Explorer 172

Websites: www.gerrardscross.gov.uk/gx/aboutgx/bulstrode

www.rspb.org.uk/reserves/guide/c/church wood/work

www.timesonline.co.uk/tol/travel/best_of_britain/article759264.ece

No book about walking in the Chilterns is complete without an excursion into the Chiltern Hundreds. Hedgerley, where the walk starts, belongs to the Burnham Hundred. Close to the start is Church Wood, an RSPB reserve. The route then goes under the M40 before entering the fine open space of Bulstrode Park which dates back to before the Norman Conquest. But there is something even older to the right as you climb — an Iron Age fort or camp. You can't see Bulstrode Camp because it is on the other side of the trees but the site can be inspected later. Also in the park is a house called Bulstrode, as Gothic as you like. The return route re-enters Church Wood before reaching Hedgerley church and the start at the White Horse.

① Walk towards the village green. Do not go up to the church but instead take the next footpath to the left.

After passing a farm you soon come to Church Wood, an RSPB reserve. You will stay on the fringes of the wood (but will go deeper at the end of the walk) before emerging into an open space.

That's the M40 in front of you. Don't worry: once past it you won't notice it

Hedgerley House with daub and wattle

Hedgerley dates from the time the early Saxon settlers moved into the southern scarp of the Chilterns. An infamous resident (but not for long) was Judge Jeffreys, the hanging judge. A more congenial local was John Hill. In 1761 Dr Hill was the first person to draw attention to the connection between tobacco and cancer. OK, it was snuff he was talking about and snuff is free of tar and harmful gases and cannot be inhaled making lung cancer impossible. Even so, John Hill was on to something. It took until 1950 before Dr Richard Doll was able to prove the link between smoking and lung cancer.

Church Wood is small, at least compared with its neighbour Burnham Beeches, but no worse for that. There are beech trees, also ash and oak; in springtime expect to see a swarm of bluebells. Naturally the birds are meant to be the stars of the show so listen for the drumming of woodpeckers and the 'tuit tuit tuit' of the nuthatch but on the day of the walk it was pheasants that were making the most racket.

House in Hedgerley Green

at all. Cross the field to meet a path coming in from the left.

2 Head for the M40 and pass under the bridge. A glance at the map tells you that you are

These days the Chiltern Hundreds has come to be associated not with real estate but with the Houses of Parliament, in particular as a procedural device to allow MPs to resign from the House of Commons (technically they are forbidden from resigning). Tony Blair for one took advantage.

definitely in the Chiltern Hundreds. Once past the M40 a road comes up, Hedgerley Lane. Go up to a house on a corner. Once there bear left between two houses to arrive in Bulstrode Park.

3 Once through a Heath Robinson sort of gate veer off slightly to the right to follow the tracks in the grass. Already the M40 seems light years away as the serenity of the surroundings begins to take a hold. The partially visible house up to the left is Bulstrode; more of that later. Over to the right is a steep rocky feature. This is Crab Hill. Behind it and through the

These days Bulstrode is the WEC

trees and undergrowth is Bulstrode Camp (see the footnote).

4 At the top of the park when you can go no further wheel obliquely left and head in a north-westerly direction along an obvious

The Bulstrode you see was completed in 1865. It replaced one built in 1686 for Bloody Judge Jeffreys. These days it is the UK headquarters of WEC (World Evangelization for Christ) International, a Christian charity.

track. Before long the ultra-Gothic spectacle of Bulstrode comes into view.

5 Cross the road as if heading for Jarretts Hill Farm but very soon take the track to the left which winds pleasantly round the northern edge of the Bulstrode Estate — note the lagoon to the right — before arriving at Hedgerley Lane.

6 Go right to cross the M40 but immediately after crossing dive down a path on the other side of the road. Make for the fence ahead before turning right to pass a house. When the drive meets a minor road turn left to reach Hedgerley Green.

7 Go right at a sign to pass the fine-looking house: Leith

At the top of Bulstrode Park

Lagoon near Bulstrode

Grove, dating from the sixteenth or early seventeenth century. At the end of the gravelled section re-enter Church Wood and continue on past a stile to arrive at the church. From there it is a short step down to the road and to the White Horse. Here is a pub that has many fans. When visited in 2010 there were eight ales on tap and 10 have been known. Then there are the real ciders.

Footnote: Concerning Bulstrode Camp there is really not a lot to see and you would need to poke about to find anything. To get to the site drive north from Hedgerley along first Village Lane then Hedgerley Lane to the junction with Windsor Road. There turn left and at the traffic lights turn left again into Oxford Road. Look out on the left for Camp Road. Park in the bay signed 'visitors' parking' (ahead are private roads) and walk down to the junction. Across and to the left is a footpath. Take the short walk to the site. Apparently 17 of the surrounding houses have parts of the fortifications in their gardens.

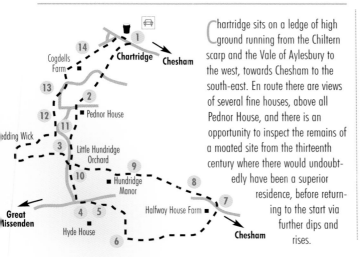

9 Chartridge and Redding Wick

Up for a characteristic Chilterns walk with more rises and falls than you can shake a stick at? This is the one.

Chartridge sits on a ledge of high ground running from the Chiltern scarp and the Vale of Aylesbury to the west, towards Chesham to the south-east. En route there are views of several fine houses, above all Pednor House, and there is an opportunity to inspect the remains of a moated site from the thirteenth century where there would undoubtedly have been a superior residence, before returning to the start via further dips and rises.

Level: 🥾🥾
Length: 7 miles
Terrain: Descents and ascents with two flat sections. Some road walking.
Park and Start: The Bell car park at Chartridge, north-west of Chesham reached by a minor road (GR 933036)
Map: OS Explorer 181
Websites: www.cheshampeople.co.uk/event/Tour-Pednor/event-5262803-detail/event
www.walkersarewelcome.org.uk

After checking that it is OK with the publican follow the footpath sign opposite the pub. Once over the stile continue half-right across a field keeping the fencing tape to your left. You are aiming for an opening beside a wall. Once there go right and then left to emerge into more open space. Admire the views over to the south. Proceed down the field to find a stile at the bottom. On the far side of the stile is a very steep descent that may be slippery, so do take care. You emerge onto a minor road known as Pednor Bottom. Go up the slope opposite then bear half right to arrive at a lane. To the left is Pednor House, well worth walking the few yards to view. With its Jacobean look (Lutyens says another pundit, no matter) it is such a handsome collection of buildings.

2 Returning to the path skirt a wall to descend a slope. At the bottom is a bridleway. Called Herbert's Hole it runs through a dry valley, not uncommon in these parts. Climb the short steep slope opposite to reach a minor road.

Pednor House

3 Turn left and walk down the road to the Chesham-Great Missenden road, on the way passing an attractive old cottage; Little Hundridge Orchard.

4 At the road cross over and turn left. Behind some gates

Old cottage

is a house approached by a long drive; this is Hyde House.

 Look for a track that goes off to the right. Head half-left towards some farm buildings. Aim just to the left of the farmyard. Go through a gate and turn left down the farmyard. At the far end cross a stile and proceed down the field leaving the good-looking farmhouse to your right.

 At the point where a house appears ahead turn left through more than 90 degrees to follow a blue bridleway arrow. You are in White's Wood, and a pleasant stroll it is. After arriving at a field continue along the bottom of the field as directed by the footpath sign until you arrive at Halfway House Farm.

White's Wood offers a pleasant stroll

7 Turn left up the road, first crossing to the opposite verge. A few yards on is a roadside memorial to two young men who lost their lives on this stretch in what was probably a head-on (viewing the scene it is impossible to ignore the injunction 'Slow' painted on the road and the arrow telling the driver to get in).

8 Turn right into the farm and then immediately left to go up a grassy slope on an obvious track. The copse over to the left is known as the Devil's Den. At the top of the slope go left to the edge of the copse and then right before turning left to continue in the same direction as before. Before long a house comes up on the left. This is Hundridge Manor. A chapel can be seen beyond the house.

Here Chesham is close. Detour into the town and you ought to get a good reception. After all Chesham is the first Walkers are Welcome town in the Chilterns.

9 Continue along the track until a sign directs you to turn right. At the bottom of the field go left and proceed along the field edge until after ascending slightly you arrive at a stile. On the other side is a minor road, the same one you were on earlier.

10 Go right up the hill again passing Little Hundridge Orchard. To the left is a footpath sign. Go through the gate and head for another gate. A wood can be seen

This site is known as Redding Wick. The moat dates from the thirteenth century. There are around 5000 moated sites known in England, most built in the period 1250 – 1350. Barons and bishops built residences on the islands created by the moats, effectively creating status symbols to dazzle the peasantry. It will be interesting if this site is preserved when the high-speed line to Birmingham goes through these parts (should the project be completed).

over to the right. Enter the wood and you are on the fringe of an earthwork with the outlines of a moat clearly visible. This is Redding Wick.

Walk through the wood to the other end then turn right. At a point where houses can be seen to the left bear half-right until you emerge from the wood. Redding's Farm is ahead of you. Walk towards it and then execute a little detour to the left to skirt the farm.

 Emerging from the farm drive turn left and walk down the stretch of road where you were briefly before. At the bottom is a road junction next to Herbert's Hole Cottage.

 Just to the left of the cottage and over to the right is a path. As you climb notice to your left a garden containing a miniature railway — an amusing diversion. At the first

Redding Wick

So what about these Pednors? Obviously they have some resonance in this area. 'Pednor' means 'Pedda's slope'. Slope is right. As for Pednor resonance how about a Tour de Pednor? There is one.

three-way junction of tracks cross a stile into a field and immediately head half-right towards a stile and a road beyond. Hop over the stile and you are at the entrance to Great Pednor Farm.

 Walk up the road keeping the farm to your left. At a bend in the road take the signed footpath. Already a sign off to the right is visible. When you get there turn right and proceed downhill to reach a bridleway.

 Cross over and go up the hill. Cogdells Farm is over to the right. Join a farm lane which turns into a residential street. At the main road turn right by the village hall and continue until you see the pub on the other side of the road.

10 The Bridgewater Monument and Aldbury Nowers

Ravishing views, a monument with its head in the sky, a village from yesteryear, a highly regarded nature reserve; all in the space of six miles: don't miss this one.

Level: 🥾

Length: 6 miles

Terrain: Undulating, no big climbs; a tiny stretch of road walking

Park and Start: If coming by car, use the free car park on the Ridgeway (GR 954148). If coming by train and therefore starting from Tring Station a note at the end explains what to do

Map: OS Explorer 181

Websites: www.hertsdirect.org/envroads/environment/countryside/walkingandriding/hertsOAL/HertsOAL/oal001

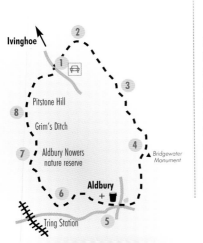

From a car park high up on the Ridgeway the walk passes through a wooded section where fine views to the west increasingly open up before arriving at the Bridgewater Monument; something to be marvelled at if only for its setting. Down the hill is Aldbury, doing a good impression of English villages of yesteryear. Next up is the Aldbury Nowers nature reserve a magnet for, among others, butterfly spotters. At the top of the reserve is Pitstone Hill; drink in the fabulous views over to the Vale of Aylesbury as well as over to Ivinghoe Beacon in the east.

59

Leave the car park and cross over the road. Over to the left the Ridgeway National Trail winds up to Ivinghoe Beacon which you will see towards the end of the walk. For now go straight ahead to what is an obvious intersection at the foot of the scarp. Once there turn right.

 Proceed up a gentle incline, at the first junction veering left. You are on the Ashridge Estate Boundary Trail. Continue up a slightly steeper incline and at the top go through a gate. There is a cottage ahead of you, Clipperdown Cottage; a kennels actually.

 Again bear left to go down by the side of the cottage. Quite soon the track will start to curve right. Some glorious views to the right begin to open up. The Bridgewater Monument and the National Trust visitor centre and teahouse are close by. It is one thing to see a picture of the monument but to quite suddenly come upon it is at once wonderful and surreal.

The monument is to Francis Egerton, the third Duke of Bridgewater, who is credited with building Britain's first canal, the Bridgewater Canal which connects Runcorn, Manchester, and Leigh. Whether 'first' is strictly correct is debatable – the Romans had a go – but it seems the Bridgewater sparked off what has been called 'canal mania'.

Looking towards Ivinghoe Beacon

Bridgewater Monument

4 To the left of the teahouse, and in the distance, is the Ashridge mansion, now a business school. The onward route lies downhill through over-arching trees, culminating in arrival at the village of Aldbury with its pond, its church, two yes two pubs, a village stores and that precious commodity – a post office. The pond is considered so stellar that the Arriva bus service carries 'Aldbury Pond' on its destination board when 'Aldbury' alone would do.

5 Leaving Aldbury by Station Road the church is soon encountered on the right. Beyond it is a track to the right running past Church Farm. Follow it for a short distance before reaching a crossing of the ways. Go left (this is the

Fine mansion in Aldbury

Hertfordshire Way) and continue again for a short distance before arriving at another cross-roads.

6 Take the right-hand fork and you are back on the Ridgeway. The trademark icon on the Ridgeway is a white acorn so if nothing else simply follow the acorns. Quite soon the route enters some

On the way to Aldbury Nowers

Aldbury Nowers, owned and managed by the National Trust, is designated a Site of Special Scientific Interest. Butterfly aficionados will be aware that it is host to Essex skippers, marbled whites, green hairstreak, brown argus, and dingy skippers. It is also a prime location for other invertebrates such as solitary bees and wasps.

woodlands; this is Aldbury Nowers, a sylvan delight.

7 Carry on upwards to a gate that marks the northern boundary of Aldbury Nowers. Now soak in the superb views over the Vale of Aylesbury. Prominent to the north is Mentmore Towers, once home of the Baron Mayer de Rothschild who moved a whole village in order to give his new house the best view. Looks like he succeeded.

8 The chalky grassy hill you are thrusting a boot up is Pitstone Hill; as you round the side of

Up to Pitstone Hill

the hill the bulk of Ivinghoe Beacon is visible straight ahead. Down to the left of the track (950143) is a micro-feature walkers in these parts are very familiar with — Grim's Ditch, that is a Grim's Ditch. Unlike some others this one is quite distinct. The views are now immense. This is truly a magical spot. Down below is an intersection of tracks. As ever the injunction is to follow the acorn. Do that and you will arrive back in the car park.

Author looking west

Note for those starting and finishing at Tring Station: Take the road east from the station using the pavement. Once across a road look for a footpath sign on the left. Follow the sign, passing a farm entrance, before arriving very quickly at the place where stage 6 of this walk commences, which means your sequence is 6-7-8-1-2-3-4-5. On completing stage 5 go left and retrace your steps to Tring Station.